I Don't Want Them to Go to Hell

50 days of encouragement for friends and families of LGBTQ people

I Don't Want Them to Go to Hell

50 days of encouragement for friends and families of LGBTQ people

Suzanne DeWitt Hall

DH Strategies

First Edition

ISBN-13: 978-0986408052
ISBN-10: 0986408050

Printed in the United States of America

DEDICATION

For my wife, who searches with me and who encourages and focuses me every, single day.

I love you, always.

CONTENTS

Introduction

My daughter Kiera was a teenager when I found out she had a girlfriend. I'd initiated a rule that she wouldn't date until she was 16, and there'd already been hints that the term "dating" had loose edges. But in my desire to protect her from the complexity of romance and the minefield of sex, I hadn't anticipated that attraction to girls would be part of the equation.

My faith formation was largely Roman Catholic, which meant I viewed same-sex relationships as "intrinsically disordered." My daughter's news kicked off several years of discussion about sexuality and gender as my daughter matured, had romantic relationships, and developed friendships with transgender people at college. The conversations were sometimes heated.

While I always wanted her to be happy, I worried she might not end up in a stable relationship. I wondered if I would ever have grandkids. I fretted over many things related to her life and mine.

All this is natural. When you find out your understanding of a loved one's gender or sexual orientation is false, you face a wide range of emotions. Those of us who come from socially conservative faith traditions worry especially about the state of our loved one's soul.

God must have giggled a bit as I worked through these issues, because he knew what was coming.

When I was 47 years old, at the end of a very dysfunctional marriage to my daughter's father, I fell in love with a woman. Diane's formation was largely Baptist, and our faith traditions both decried homosexuality. We met in church, became friends, led ministry, and prayed together for our families. Then after a while, the relationship shifted into more, much to our puzzlement. It made no sense; we were both devout with conservative views regarding sexuality.

My wife's mother struggled with the news. "Does that mean you're no longer a Christian?" she asked. The question was painful, because Diane's faith never shifted. Her mother had always known her to be devoted to Jesus, and seen her consistently turn to prayer, looking to God to guide and keep her. Diane was devastated by her family's response, even though she understood it because she'd held the same views.

As time passed, Diane's mom came to see the way God shines through our love for each other. She even attended our wedding. There's much she still doesn't understand, but her fears about Diane going to hell have subsided.

Your fears can subside too.

It turned out my daughter was a prophet who tried to speak truths to me at a time I wasn't able to hear them. The person in your life who trusted you enough to share the truth about their sexual orientation or gender identity now plays that role for you. I hope you can be more open to it than I was.

God is watching as you work your way to a new understanding of your loved one, and cheering you on. He desires wholeness for each of us and for our relationships with each other, and is glad you've picked up this book as part of your search.

Throughout the scriptures God tells us "Do not be afraid." May God's comfort, love, and revelation pour out to you as you contemplate each day's devotional reading, and may your heart be open to receive those things, and more.

Guide to Translations

People with concerns about their loved ones come from widely ranging denominational affiliations. This devotional therefore includes a variety of Bible translations to reflect that diversity. Acronyms for included versions are listed below.

ASV	American Standard Version
ESV	English Standard Version
KJV	King James Version
NAB	New American Bible
NABRE	New American Bible Revised Edition
NASB	New American Standard Bible
NIV	New International Version
NKJV	New King James Version
NRSV	New Revised Standard Version
NRSVCE	New Revised Standard Version Catholic Edition
RSV	Revised Standard Version

First, the Basics

There are many topics you'll want to explore after a loved one trusts you enough to share the truth about their sexual orientation or gender identity. You probably want to jump right into the issues of sexuality and gender, but instead we are going to start with the fundamentals: God, the Bible, Law, and the things Jesus condemns.

We start there because all other questions rest upon them.

WHO IS GOD?

Our view of God directs the way we view scripture, and so before we go any further we will contemplate the one who breathed life into the collection of books which make up the Bible.

This section is critical because all that follows hinges on who we know God to be. Jesus tells us when we see him, we see the Father. Jesus is the full revelation of God. That means understanding scripture, relationships, and the world around us all center on this central question.

Who is God?

DAY 1: GOD IS LOVE

*Everyone who loves has been born of God and knows God. Whoever does
not love does not know God, because God is love.*
(1 John 4:7-8, NIV)

As you read through scripture, you can find God described as merciful,
jealous, compassionate, angry, and forgiving. These adjectives describe
God's attributes and responses. But they don't say who God *is*. John's
statement above stands out from all the other descriptors in a very
powerful way, because it doesn't describe a characteristic or emotion.
It proclaims God's very being.

John doesn't say "God is *loving*." He says "God *is* love." That's a
world of difference.

Remember the author of the passage is the beloved disciple. The
one who reclined at Jesus' side and laid his head on Jesus' shoulder at
that final supper. The only male who stood beneath the cross as Jesus
suffered and died. The one to whom Jesus entrusted the care of his
mother. It can be argued that of all the apostles, John knew Jesus best.

Let's look at John's wonderful proclamation again: "Everyone
who loves has been born of God and knows God."

What a powerfully inclusive statement.

A famous hymn written by James Quinn called *Here in Christ we
Gather* contains the following refrain:

> "God is love, and where true love is
> God himself is there."

We are formed in the image and likeness of our creator, and we are
called to love. True love is not selfish or judgmental. It is not focused
on sex acts. It crosses all genders, races, physical and emotional
handicaps, sexual orientations, and other labels designed to create
separation between humans. True love springs from God and unites
us all into oneness with the beautiful image and likeness of Christ.

3

Where true love is, God himself is there.

Deep within my existence something said, without any words, "This is what life is supposed to be. You were created to feel deeply and love deeply, without doubt, without shame, and without guilt."
Tim Rymel

Day 2: Father and Giver of Good Gifts

Is there anyone among you who, if your child asks for bread, will give a stone? Or if the child asks for a fish, will give a snake? If you then, who are evil, know how to give good gifts to your children, how much more will your Father in heaven give good things to those who ask him!
(Matthew 7:9-11 NRSV)

In this small segment near the end of Jesus' long set of instructions delivered from a mountaintop, we get a glimpse of the generosity of God's response to our requests. He reminds us the Holy One in heaven is not some authoritarian, disinterested wrath bearer. Rather, he is *Father*.

The child described in this passage is asking only for sustenance: bread and fish. But many things are needed for us to be healthy, functioning human beings. Maslow's hierarchy of human needs tells us once we are fed we require safety. And once we are safe we require being loved and belonging. And once we belong, we need to be respected. And only once we have these things do we have any chance of becoming fully the people God designed us to be.

Through Maslow's groundbreaking research, it has become widely understood that humans need much more than just food to survive. Our God, Creator and Father, knows this as well, for he is the master designer of humanity.

Who is God? He is our Father. The one to whom we can turn with our requests for acceptance, for belonging, for safety, and for respect. God is the giver of good gifts.

He died not for men, but for each man. If each man had been the only man made, He would have done no less.
C.S. Lewis

DAY 3:   LIKE US IN EVERY RESPECT

*Since, therefore, the children share flesh and blood, he himself likewise
shared the same things, so that through death he might destroy the one who
has the power of death, that is, the devil, and free those who all their lives
were held in slavery by the fear of death. For it is clear that he did not
come to help angels, but the descendants of Abraham. Therefore he had to
become like his brothers and sisters in every respect, so that he might be a
merciful and faithful high priest in the service of God, to make a sacrifice
of atonement for the sins of the people. Because he himself was tested by
what he suffered, he is able to help those who are being tested.*
(Hebrews 2:14-18 NRSV)

Did you catch that? Jesus is like us in *every* respect.

Don't brush this sentence off casually. Let it sink in, deep to the
core of who you are. God is like us in *every* respect. He is like the
transgender woman who is worried she'll be murdered while walking
to her car after work. He is like the broken-hearted gay man who
can't attend the church of his childhood. He is like the bisexual
intersex person who doesn't conform to gender norms and endures
the snide looks and sniggers of strangers. He is like these people just
as much as the heterosexual man who is comfortable performing his
gender in a way this society finds acceptable.

Imagine what it would have been like in the ancient Middle East
to feel gender ambiguity and be afraid to act on it. Imagine the
difficulty of not showing sexual attraction to both genders. Because
he was like us in every respect, he was like each of the people
described above. Jesus' reality was like theirs.

Jesus understands the difficulty of being LGBTQ and cries for his
siblings' pain. Remember that when you offer comfort and aid to one
such as this, you offer it to Christ, himself.

*There is nothing we can do to make God love us more; there is nothing we
can do to make God love us less.*
Philip Yancey

WHAT IS THE BIBLE?

God is love as revealed through the person of Jesus, a person who is like us in all ways. With that understanding in mind, we now look at the Bible itself. What is it? How are we to view it?

The Holy Spirit whispered the messages of the Bible to the writers who captured them. But the Bible is not God. Our Creator wants us to worship him alone, and the Trinity can never be constrained to a box the size of a book on your bedside table.

Evaluating your understanding of the nature of scripture does not threaten the reality of God or your relationship with him. If it does, you are worshipping the Bible rather than Jesus Christ.

Over the next week we'll ask the Spirit to help us gain a proper, Godly perspective on the collection of books we call the Bible.

DAY 4:   OPENABLE ONLY BY JESUS

*I saw a scroll in the right hand of the one who sat on the throne. It had
writing on both sides and was sealed with seven seals. Then I saw a mighty
angel who proclaimed in a loud voice, "Who is worthy to open the scroll and
break its seals?" But no one in heaven or on earth or under the earth was able
to open the scroll or to examine it. I shed many tears because no one was found
worthy to open the scroll or to examine it. One of the elders said to me, "Do
not weep. The lion of the tribe of Judah, the root of David, has triumphed,
enabling him to open the scroll with its seven seals." Then I saw standing in
the midst of the throne and the four living creatures and the elders a Lamb
that seemed to have been slain. He had seven horns and seven eyes; these are
the [seven] spirits of God sent out into the whole world. He came and received
the scroll from the right hand of the one who sat on the throne. When he took
it, the four living creatures and the twenty-four elders fell down before the
Lamb. Each of the elders held a harp and gold bowls filled with incense,
which are the prayers of the holy ones. They sang a new hymn:*

*"Worthy are you to receive the scroll and to break open its seals, for you were
slain and with your blood you purchased for God those from every tribe and
tongue, people and nation."* (Revelation 5:1-9 NABRE)

We start our exploration of the scriptures by going to the very end.
John's mystical visioning in Revelation reveals the very heart of the
issue:

No one in heaven or on earth is able to open the scriptures. We can
only peer at the scrolls from behind our various veils and see darkly
what is written there. There is only one who is worthy and able, and
that is the Lamb of God.

Unless we filter all of our contemplation of the Hebrew and
Christian scriptures through the person of Christ, the words are
impenetrable. And as our first devotion informed us, the person of
Jesus is love. We will revisit this truth throughout this book, because
it is the key to every scriptural question.

> *"No text can be understood out of its entire context. The most 'entire'
> context is Jesus."*
> Eugene H. Peterson

Day 5: Capable of Giving Wisdom

But you must continue in the things which you have learned and been assured of, knowing from whom you have learned them, and that from childhood you have known the Holy Scriptures, which are able to make you wise for salvation through faith which is in Christ Jesus. All Scripture is given by inspiration of God, and is profitable for doctrine, for reproof, for correction, for instruction in righteousness, that the man of God may be complete, thoroughly equipped for every good work. (2 Timothy 3:14-17 NKJV)

Paul is held up by many Evangelicals as the supreme authority on who we are to be as Christians. Some of us talk as if his statements are more important than those of Jesus himself. Certain circles claim that The Word of God and the word of God are one and the same. But in taking this position, they defy Paul's instructions to his beloved Timothy, above. For nowhere does Paul say the Bible and Jesus are essentially the same, and certainly not in today's passage though it is often used in defense of that position.

What Paul *does* say is this: the Holy Scriptures are able to make you wise, though only through faith in Jesus. And the scriptures are profitable, instructive, and useful for equipping us for good work. With these things all Christians can agree.

If *The Word* and *the word* are the same, why didn't Paul point it out to the disciple he loved so much, when he instructed him on how to lead? Surely this would have been important to know for the man who would become the first Bishop of Ephesus.

Self is the opaque veil that hides the face of God from us. It can be removed only in spiritual experience, never by mere instruction.
A. W. Tozer

DAY 6: INCAPABLE OF PROVIDING ETERNAL LIFE

You search the scriptures, because you think you have eternal life through them; even they testify on my behalf. But you do not want to come to me to have life. (John 5:39-40 NABRE)

Today's passage shows us the more things change, the more they stay the same. The verses come from a discourse Jesus offers after the Jews plot to kill him for breaking the Sabbath and for claiming to be the son of God. He tells them flat out that while they think they can find their salvation through the scriptures, they are wrong.

The religious conservatives of the day knew the scriptures inside and out. They knew the predictions about the messiah and yet when he stood before them, they didn't think he matched their scriptural understanding. They didn't expect him to do things like violate Jewish law, or proclaim Samaritans and Roman pagans had greater faith than they did, or interrupt the righteous stoning of a woman caught in adultery. This was *not* the kind of messiah they anticipated. They wanted the thing they *did* expect; a triumphant king who would kick the Romans out of Jerusalem and be a good and faithful Jew like David. The religious authorities were so outraged by the Jesus who stood in front of them they decided he had to die.

The reason the gospel accounts are important is not merely that they tell us what happened during the days Jesus walked the earth. They are also important because they show us these things are still happening today. Many of us scour the Bible to sculpt a messiah which fits our own ideas of justice, despite the Jesus who sits before us in stories of outrageous, inclusive, love. We proclaim that an inclusive Jesus is fiction, and the real Jesus has eyes of fire and wields a sword of righteous damnation. And like the Jews who demanded the life of Christ, we demand eternal life can only be found through the scriptures and all its accompanying law. Like them, we do not seem to want to come to Jesus to have life. We want to come to the *image* of Jesus we construct from a subset of scriptural passages. The image that matches our view of what he should look and act like.

If Jesus were to walk around with us today, he would undoubtedly be killed again for not matching the image we construct. Like the Jews described in the John 5 passage, too many of us are not willing to look to the radical nature of love as the source for eternal life.

This earth indeed is the very Body of God, and it is from this body that we are born, live, suffer, and resurrect to eternal life. Either all is God's Great Project, or we may rightly wonder whether anything is God's Great Project. One wonders if we humans will be the last to accept this.
Richard Rohr

DAY 7: A COLLECTION OF VARYINGLY IMPORTANT PASSAGES

Blessed is the one who keeps the words of the prophecy of this book.
(Revelation 22:7 ESV)

Revelation is one of the trippiest, most difficult, and perhaps even incomprehensible books of the Bible. How can we possibly keep the words of all the prophecy contained within it when we don't have a clue what it means?

Many Christians claim that all scripture has equal value for our salvation. But the reality is we must apply varying weights and values to different passages and even entire books. How many of us turn to the genealogy listings for comfort or guidance? How many turn to the census data included in Numbers? Are pages full of names as useful to us as the parables Jesus unfolded? Do they help govern our passions the way Paul counsels in the epistles? Do they offer insight into the passionate love God holds for us the way Solomon professes in his Song of Songs?

It's perfectly okay to acknowledge that some passages are more important than others in the scriptures. If it weren't so, why would we need Jesus' words printed in red as is common in many Bibles?

We can believe in the God-breathed nature and inerrancy of the scriptures and still consider some books to be more insightful about the person of Christ and God himself. We need not demand that every sentence be equally important. We don't have to expect to understand every troubling vision experienced by John or Daniel, and try to "keep" it. It's just not possible.

What we *must* do is hold on to the revelation of the person of Christ; the One who is the way, the truth, and the life. And that way, that truth, and that life, is love.

The death penalty is "biblical" in the same way that war, slavery, and the oppression of women are "biblical." Biblical, but not like Jesus.
Nathan Hamm

Day 8:   Written by Errant People

But to the rest I, not the Lord, say: If any brother has a wife who does not believe, and she is willing to live with him, let him not divorce her.
(1 Corinthians 7:12 NKJV)

Now concerning virgins: I have no commandment from the Lord; yet I give judgment as one whom the Lord in His mercy has made trustworthy.
(1 Corinthians 7:25 NKJV)

What I speak, I speak not according to the Lord, but as it were, foolishly, in this confidence of boasting. (2 Corinthians 11:17 NKJV)

The doctrine of inerrancy is extremely important to many Christians who worry about the salvation of their LGBTQ loved ones. Here's how one Roman Catholic document describes inerrancy:

Since, therefore, all that the inspired authors, or sacred writers, affirm should be regarded as affirmed by the Holy Spirit, we must acknowledge that the books of Scripture firmly, faithfully and without error teach that truth which God, for the sake of our salvation, wished to see confided to the sacred Scriptures.

Some Christians believe inerrancy applies only to the original manuscripts, while others contend it has been passed along through millennia of replications and translations. Still others demand inerrancy only exists in the King James Version. It's an interesting argument, but not one we will take on here.

Look at Paul's words in the passages from the two letters to the Corinthians. In each of these verses, Paul makes it clear he is writing his *own* thoughts, not God's. This introduces a significant logic challenge. If every word in the Bible is inerrant, then what he says *must* be true and therefore the words do not come from God. But if all scripture is God breathed and therefore comes from God, then Paul's words are false.

Which is it?

Paul writes to the new Christians in Corinth who have found themselves fractured between teachers who demand different sets of rules be followed. You can almost hear him sighing as he writes, frustrated at the state they are in and their lack of teeth for chewing spiritual meat. He pours out milk in the form of verbal slaps, periodically sweetened with a sprinkle of encouragement. He undoubtedly strove to write what was true and passed along what he thought the Corinthians needed to hear. But just as some people confuse the Bible with God Himself, some people confuse the inerrancy of scripture with the inerrancy of the individual writers. In chapter 7, Paul is so convinced the end is coming soon that he urges people not to marry. He was wrong about that. He was in error. It's thousands of years later, and we are still waiting for Christ to come again.

Can Paul's words be wrong yet still inerrant? For the purposes he was trying to accomplish at that time, yes. But are they the fullness of truth, for all times, places, and situations? No. The epistles were penned by people who did their best to capture the messages of the Holy Spirit, to people who they assumed wanted to conform to the mind of Christ. But those people were not perfect at either end. They were imperfect people writing to imperfect people about perfect truth. Writing *at* that time, *for* that time, without error.

Millennia later we read Paul's words in chapter 11 about how it is a disgrace for men to have long hair, and for women to pray with their head uncovered. We disregard those passages, considering them to be irrelevant artifacts of a bygone culture. We continue in the same chapter, reading the words of the institution of communion, and see them as beautiful words and timelessly applicable. Both views are true.

The concept of inerrancy is a mystery which we cannot solve here on earth. But key to managing the lack of answers is that Jesus didn't leave us a book; he left us a group of followers which we call church. He didn't feed us a book; he fed us himself. He never demanded rigid adherence to a book; he reproved those who did.

We can believe in the God-breathed truth of the scriptures without insisting each line be applied literally to our lives today. And most assuredly, Jesus does not want the idea of inerrancy to be used as a weapon against our fellow brothers and sisters in Christ.

There's a lovely Hasidic story of a rabbi who always told his people that if they studied the Torah, it would put Scripture on their hearts. One of them asked, "Why on our hearts, and not in them?" The rabbi answered, "Only God can put Scripture inside. But reading sacred text can put it on your heart, and then when your hearts break, the holy words will fall inside."

Anne Lamott

DAY 9:   LOVE STORY NOT HAMMER

Genesis 19:1-25
Leviticus 18:22 and 20:13
1 Corinthians 6:9-11
1 Timothy 1:9-10
Jude 6-7
Romans 1:25-27

There's a pretty good chance most of your fear and concern about LGBTQ loved ones come from these passages. So go ahead and count them.

There are just seven "clobber" passages containing 37 verses out of a Bible made up of over 31,000 verses.

A host of wonderful resources are available for addressing each of these passages in detail, so we won't be doing that today. Instead, we're discussing how small these bits of the Bible are in comparison to the whole.

The Hebrew Scriptures which Christians call the Old Testament are peppered with calls from the prophets to honor God by doing justice, practicing mercy, and being faithful to him. They speak of a God who never stops chasing us, and who always receives us back when we falter. They include just a few mentions of homosexual behavior, all of which have contextual settings which must be studied to be properly understood. New Testament clobber passages have similar cultural context which also requires exploration.

In the gospels, we see numerous stories of Jesus welcoming people who were disdained by religious experts. Those stories not only outnumber the clobber passages, they outweigh them in importance when trying to understand what it means to follow Christ. After all, they include the words and actions of God himself, in the person of Christ.

Notice that not a single one of the clobber verses are the words of Jesus.

16

The Bible as a whole proclaims God's demand for justice, mercy, and love. Don't let a handful of passages stripped of context outweigh the thrust of the Bible with its grand culmination of Good News.

It's supposed to be a love story, not a hammer.

> *The Bible, it is presumed, gives a definitive answer to the question "is homosexuality a sin." If that were the case, then one would expect to find both a quantity and quality of passages in the Scriptures that effectively and clearly support such a proposition.... For if we (the church) are going to assume such a position (that homosexuality is a sin) then we should probably make sure the Biblical ground we are standing on is secure.*
> Rev. Colby Martin

DAY 10: ICON NOT IDOL

Thou shalt not make unto thee a graven image, nor any likeness of any thing that is in heaven above, or that is in the earth beneath, or that is in the water under the earth (Exodus 20:4 ASV)

Icons are an ancient form of artwork designed to be windows into heaven via prayer. They aren't meant to be so much looked *at* as *through* to behold the glorious mysteries of God. This is what the Bible should be, but often isn't. Instead, a good number of Christians conflate Jesus and the Bible. The premise is based on the opening sentence in John's gospel:

In the beginning was the Word, and the Word was with God, and the Word was God. (John 1:1 ASV)

But there's a huge difference between the Word who is God himself, and the word which we call the scriptures. The very last sentence of John's gospel makes this reality clear:

And there are also many other things which Jesus did, the which if they should be written every one, I suppose that even the world itself would not contain the books that should be written. (John 21:25 ASV)

John tells us just the things Jesus *did* would fill so many books the world could not contain them. And that's only his actions! Actions offer just one avenue of insight into the reality of a being. Through them we can see much, but not the whole. And our God is Triune; three persons, one God. So through the God-breathed, inerrant words of John we know a world filled with books could not describe what Jesus did. This means there is no possible way a single volume we call the Bible can be the same as God himself.

It's simply not possible.

Nowhere in scripture does it say Jesus *is* the Bible. He is the Word, and the Bible is his inspired word. But those two are not the same things. We must be very careful not to believe the two are one, because doing so turns the Bible into an idol.

The scriptures should be an icon of God; a window through which we can enter into his mystical reality. But by no means should we turn the Bible into a graven image.

> *"Concepts create idols; only wonder comprehends anything. People kill one another over idols. Wonder makes us fall to our knees."*
> Gregory of Nyssa

LET'S TALK ABOUT LAW

Many of us fear that our LGBTQ loved ones violate scriptural injunctions. But it turns out the law is a tricky thing, which the words and actions of Jesus make clear. Over the coming days we'll look at scriptures in which Jesus informs us about how Christians should view Biblical law.

In doing so we discover that Jesus frequently broke Jewish law, that Old Testament law was problematic in many ways, and that love is the fulfillment of the law.

All of this is very good news.

DAY 11: JESUS BREAKS THE SABBATH REPEATEDLY

And this was why the Jews were persecuting Jesus, because he was doing these things on the Sabbath. But Jesus answered them, "My Father is working until now, and I am working." This was why the Jews were seeking all the more to kill him, because not only was he breaking the Sabbath, but he was even calling God his own Father, making himself equal with God. (John 5:16-18 ESV)

When trying to wrap your head around the idea that being an LGBTQ Christian is okay, it's important to remember something extremely significant: Jesus himself broke the law. Numerous times.

The Sabbath was so important in the Old Testament that it's even included in the Ten Commandments. Rules relating to it are outlined in Leviticus, Deuteronomy, Numbers, and other books. Numbers 15:32-36 tells the story of a man who collected firewood on the Sabbath being taken out of the camp and stoned to death as punishment. Clearly, violating the rules for inactivity on the Lord's Day was a big deal.

Then here comes Jesus, who breaks Sabbath rules repeatedly. In today's passage we see that the Jews were ready to dole out the punishment required by law for his insolence.

We know the law was made for humans rather than for God. But that doesn't change the reality of Jesus' actions. They were intentional violations.

Jesus broke the law. Indisputably. For his own reasons: to establish a new order for those of us in the kingdom who still walk around on the earth, and to show us love is more important than law.

It is no coincidence that Christian fundamentalist movements worldwide seek a return to Old Testament laws - because they fundamentally reject Christ as the New Covenant - which replaced all that. They are not Christians—they are Leviticans.
Christina Engela

Day 12: Jesus Violates Purification Laws

And there was a woman who had had a discharge of blood for twelve years, and who had suffered much under many physicians, and had spent all that she had, and was no better but rather grew worse. She had heard the reports about Jesus and came up behind him in the crowd and touched his garment. For she said, "If I touch even his garments, I will be made well." And immediately the flow of blood dried up, and she felt in her body that she was healed of her disease. And Jesus, perceiving in himself that power had gone out from him, immediately turned about in the crowd and said, "Who touched my garments?" And his disciples said to him, "You see the crowd pressing around you, and yet you say, 'Who touched me?'" And he looked around to see who had done it. But the woman, knowing what had happened to her, came in fear and trembling and fell down before him and told him the whole truth. And he said to her, "Daughter, your faith has made you well; go in peace, and be healed of your disease."
(Mark 5:25-34 ESV)

The brave woman who approached Jesus in this story broke religious law. Instructions for menstruating women listed in Leviticus 15 included isolation so they would not cause others to become ritually impure. She would have been housebound for years because of this unexplained and incurable issue of blood. Her life would have been severely curtailed as she was stuck within the confines of the walls of her home.

But out she goes into the crowd, having heard Jesus was passing through town, and hoping and praying he might heal her. She compounds her "sinfulness" by touching his garment, despite knowing she was defiling him in the process.

It was not her fault that she had been bleeding for years. It was governed by some internal mystery of organs and hormones, and was not fixable despite her efforts to try and change it. The same thing is true for LGBTQ people. Their gender and sexual orientation is not something controllable or chosen. It cannot be "fixed" through conversion therapy or stern biblical admonitions. It simply is. These people should not be confined to closets as this woman with the issue of blood had been.

It was not her strict adherence to the rites and rituals of religion that made her whole. It was her faith. And that faith allowed her to go in peace.

Meanwhile, Jesus continued along his way to resurrect the dead daughter of a religious official, despite knowing he'd been made ritually unclean. He did not stop for ritual purification. He went on, in violation of the law, to continue his ministry.

Jesus was consistently on the side of those who were outcast by society and bore the unfair burden of disdain, discrimination, and prejudice. It is likely that he would look at modern-day lesbian, gay, bisexual, and transgender people and hold real sympathy for them and their plight. He would have understood the implications of a system set up to benefit the heterosexual majority over the homosexual minority. It is hard to imagine Jesus joining in the wholesale discrimination against LGBT people. Isn't it logical that he would be sympathetic to young gay teens who take their own lives rather than live with the stigma attached to their sexual orientation? Would he not be found speaking a word of support, encouragement, and hope to them? Would he not be seeking a change in the hearts of those who treat them as outcasts?
The Right Reverend Gene Robinson

Day 13: The letter kills

Not that we are sufficient of ourselves to think of anything as being from ourselves, but our sufficiency is from God, who also made us sufficient as ministers of the new covenant, not of the letter but of the Spirit; for the letter kills, but the Spirit gives life.
(2 Corinthians 3:5-6 NKJV)

The Pharisees most often mentioned in the gospels are the ones who wielded the law like a scythe to cut down those who didn't follow every jot and tittle. Of course no one *could* obey the letter of the law completely, which is why Christ came; to fulfill it. Many modern day Christians still demand such obedience, though we pick and choose which laws are okay to be discarded. Many see it as a noble duty, a supreme calling from God himself, just as Paul no doubt did at the stoning of Stephen in Acts chapter 7.

But look at these glorious words from Paul, whose writing often wavers between his Pharisaical training and the wonderful new freedom of Christ. He tells us our "sufficiency," our "enoughness," doesn't come from straining to follow the letter of the law. It doesn't even say we are to follow the *spirit* of the law. He says our sufficiency, our adequacy, comes from Christ. Not only that; he reports that God equips us to be ministers of the Spirit.

Jesus doesn't make us sufficient so we can be law-wielders. After all, Paul tells us the letter *kills*. When we wield the law as modern day Pharisees, it is a weapon of death.

Christians are not supposed to be death wielders. We are called to be ministers of the life-giving Spirit.

The dying thief had, perhaps, disobeyed the will of God in many things: but in the most important event of his life he listened and obeyed. The Pharisees had kept the law to the letter and had spent their lives in the pursuit of a most scrupulous perfection. But they were so intent upon perfection as an abstraction that when God manifested His will and His perfection in a concrete and definite way they had no choice but to reject it.
Thomas Merton

DAY 14: LAW IS TOO HEAVY TO CARRY

One of the experts in the law answered him, "Teacher, when you say these things, you insult us also." Jesus replied, "And you experts in the law, woe to you, because you load people down with burdens they can hardly carry, and you yourselves will not lift one finger to help them. "Woe to you, because you build tombs for the prophets, and it was your ancestors who killed them. So you testify that you approve of what your ancestors did; they killed the prophets, and you build their tombs. Because of this, God in his wisdom said, 'I will send them prophets and apostles, some of whom they will kill and others they will persecute.' Therefore this generation will be held responsible for the blood of all the prophets that has been shed since the beginning of the world, from the blood of Abel to the blood of Zechariah, who was killed between the altar and the sanctuary. Yes, I tell you, this generation will be held responsible for it all.
(Luke 11:45-51 NIV)

Oh, the power of that very first sentence!

Jesus, the fulfillment of the Hebrew Scripture's prophecy and law, appears among the religious experts, hoping they will have ears to hear his transformative, radical proclamation of love. In response, they are insulted. How dare a humble carpenter from the insignificant town of Nazareth try to teach them anything about God?

How dare a queer young man living in an ultraconservative small town in the Bible belt? How dare a transgender woman of color? How dare the devout Catholic mother of a daughter who just came out as lesbian?

Those ancient experts in the law approved of the way their ancestors treated the prophets of the day; killing and persecuting them so they wouldn't have to listen to messages of repentance. Some of us today do the same; implying our moral superiority while condemning voices of tolerance, acceptance, and love.

LGBTQ people are persecuted and sometimes even murdered just for trying to live their lives authentically. Those lives can never be restored. It will be hard to find comfort if that happens to someone you love. The religious experts who contribute to those deaths through hateful rhetoric and rejection will be held responsible for the bloodshed.

Woe be it to them.

Let's make sure their story isn't also ours.

Moral courage is a rarer commodity than bravery in battle or great intelligence. Yet it is the one essential, vital quality of those who seek to change a world which yields most painfully to change.
Robert F. Kennedy

DAY 15: JESUS' COMMANDMENTS TRUMP ALL LAW

When the Pharisees heard that he had silenced the Sadducees, they gathered together, and one of them, a lawyer, asked him a question to test him. "Teacher, which commandment in the law is the greatest?" He said to him, "'You shall love the Lord your God with all your heart, and with all your soul, and with all your mind. This is the greatest and first commandment. And a second is like it: 'You shall love your neighbor as yourself.' On these two commandments hang all the law and the prophets."
(Matthew 22:34-40 RSV)

Then one of the scribes came, and having heard them reasoning together, perceiving that He had answered them well, asked Him, "Which is the first commandment of all?" Jesus answered him, "The first of all the commandments is: 'Hear, O Israel, the Lord our God, the Lord is one. And you shall love the Lord your God with all your heart, with all your soul, with all your mind, and with all your strength.' This is the first commandment. And the second, like it, is this: 'You shall love your neighbor as yourself.' There is no other commandment greater than these."
(Mark 12:28-31 NKJV)

Many Bibles print the words of Jesus in red, and with a quick scan we can see how much of the text is made up of his speech. The gospels include a great deal of red ink; much of it instructions for how to get to heaven. Some of these instructions appear to be conflicting, and have led to fierce arguments among Christians which ultimately resulted in denominational splits. But in today's passage we look at the word "commandment."

It is a special word, one which is not used all that much in our scriptures. You will generally find it only in reference to the words stamped on the tablets Moses bore down the mountain, and to verses like today's.

That should make us pay attention. We find Jesus using the phrase "command" and "commandment" rarely, and when he does, it is always in a similar context to the above. It is always a command to love.

"Command" has a very special meaning. It is not the same as to instruct, or urge, or proclaim, or exhort. It stands alone in virtue of its concrete, authoritative, definitive nature. It is very close in meaning to the word "demand."

The Ten Commandments trumped all the other laws and rules developed over time as delivered by Moses or developed by the religious authorities. And the commandments of Jesus override everything which came before.

And so I discovered that it is not on our forgiveness any more than on our goodness that the world's healing hinges, but on His. When He tells us to love our enemies, He gives, along with the command, the love itself.
Corrie ten Boom

DAY 16: JESUS FULFILLS THE LAW

"Do not think that I have come to abolish the law or the prophets; I have come not to abolish but to fulfill. For truly I tell you, until heaven and earth pass away, not one letter, not one stroke of a letter, will pass from the law until all is accomplished." (Matthew 5:17-18 NRSV)

Today we examine a phrase which you've probably heard in criticisms of LGBTQ individuals. It's from Jesus' words about neither jot nor tittle passing away, which is used as a demand that the law somehow remains through him, unchanged. Many good Christians earnestly believe that his statement about fulfillment means things are to stay the same. But this thinking skips the critical phrase that follows, which reads "...until all is accomplished."

And guess what? It all *has* been accomplished, at least according to John.

John 4:34 *My food is to do the will of the one who sent me and to* **finish** *his work.*

John 17:4 *I glorified you on earth by* **accomplishing** *the work that you gave me to do.*

John 19:28 *After this, aware that everything was now* **finished***, in order that the scripture might be fulfilled, Jesus said, "I thirst."*

John 19:30 *When Jesus had taken the wine, he said, "It is* **finished***." And bowing his head, he handed over the spirit.*

Jesus was the fulfillment of the law, not its replacement, just as he says. But the good news is that everything *has been accomplished*, through him.

Struggling against the legalism of simple obedience, we end by setting up the most dangerous law of all, the law of the world and the law of grace. In our effort to combat legalism we land ourselves in the worst kind of legalism. The only way of overcoming this legalism is by real obedience to Christ when he calls us to follow him; for in Jesus the law is at once fulfilled and cancelled.
Dietrich Bonhoeffer

Day 17: Love is the Fulfilling of the Law

Owe no one anything, except to love each other, for the one who loves another has fulfilled the law. For the commandments, "You shall not commit adultery, You shall not murder, You shall not steal, You shall not covet," and any other commandment, are summed up in this word: "You shall love your neighbor as yourself." Love does no wrong to a neighbor; therefore love is the fulfilling of the law. (Romans 13:8-10 ESV)

Paul weaves in and out of legalism which is understandable given his training. But in this passage, his words echo those of Jesus pretty directly.

It's a passage which hardly warrants any additional commentary. You could simply read this three times, spend a few minutes in contemplation, and be done.

Love is the fulfilling of the law. Such simple words, and powerful truth. In applying this truth, many of us are taught that love means not leaving a friend in what we perceive to be sin.

But how is it loving, under any circumstance, to tell someone they shouldn't be who they were born to be? How loving is it to tell a desperately lonely woman who is in fear of hell that she should remain alone forever rather than marry the person who has brought wholeness to her being for the first time in her life? How is it loving to tell a teenager they can't perform gender in the way that is natural to them because their external sex characteristics don't match that gender?

Many Bible passages indicate slavery is socially acceptable. Would it be loving to tell a person held in slavery that God desires their suffering rather than their freedom? That's exactly what we do to our LGBTQ loved ones when we tell them to deny who God created them to be. And it is wrong.

Paul reiterates Jesus' commandments to love one another. So go out and live the golden rule, and by doing so, fulfill the law. Treat your LGBTQ loved ones the way you want to be treated.

What religion do I preach? The religion of love. The law of kindness brought to light by the gospel. What is this good for? To make all who receive it enjoy God and themselves, to make them like God, lovers of all, contented in their lives, and crying out at their death, in calm assurance, "O grave where is thy victory! Thanks be to God, who giveth me victory, through my Lord Jesus Christ."
John Wesley

Day 18: Law Creates Unholy Zeal

Brothers and sisters, my heart's desire and prayer to God for the Israelites is that they may be saved. For I can testify about them that they are zealous for God, but their zeal is not based on knowledge. Since they did not know the righteousness of God and sought to establish their own, they did not submit to God's righteousness. Christ is the culmination of the law so that there may be righteousness for everyone who believes.
(Romans 10:1-4 NIV)

How interesting that Paul prayed for the Israelites to be saved! He knew their zeal first hand, having been among the most zealous of the faithful. They strived so hard to follow the rules and regulations of Jewish law and tradition, fervently believing doing so would earn them entrance into God's kingdom.

But Paul's words contain an interestingly subtle point. He says they would not *submit* to God's righteousness. This connotes pride, because submission requires humility. The zealous often have difficulty in this area. The zeal of the Israelites was marked by certainty sprung not from faith in God, but from faith in the correctness of their particular interpretation of scripture. They sought a righteousness of their own creation.

We moderns do the same.

So how do we overcome this susceptibility?

First, seek to *know* God. Studying the scriptures can help, but remember you don't form relationships by reading. Relationship comes from interaction. Pray. Talk to God. Ask for revelation from the Holy Spirit.

Second, seek to know *God* rather than a set of rules. When you look to the scriptures for insight, remember the Father sent the Son as the *fullness of revelation* about his being. Look therefore to Jesus for the most complete scriptural picture.

Third, repeat Paul's final sentence in this passage:

Christ is the culmination of the law so that there may be righteousness for everyone who believes.

Christ is the culmination of the law. Righteousness comes not through slavish obedience to rules, but through belief in him. Rest in this, and pray for zealous Christians just as Paul prayed for the zealous Israelites.

Especially if that zealousness applies to you.

You think that your laws correct evil - they only increase it. There is but one way to end evil - by rendering good for evil to all men without distinction.
Leo Tolstoy

Day 19: Loving God and Neighbor is Fulfillment of the Law

So the scribe said to Him, "Well said, Teacher. You have spoken the truth, for there is one God, and there is no other but He. And to love Him with all the heart, with all the understanding, with all the soul, and with all the strength, and to love one's neighbor as oneself, is more than all the whole burnt offerings and sacrifices."
Now when Jesus saw that he answered wisely, He said to him, "You are not far from the kingdom of God." (Mark 12:32-34 NKJV)

And behold, a certain lawyer stood up and tested Him, saying, "Teacher, what shall I do to inherit eternal life?" He said to him, "What is written in the law? What is your reading of it?" So he answered and said, "'You shall love the Lord your God with all your heart, with all your soul, with all your strength, and with all your mind,' and 'your neighbor as yourself.'" And He said to him, "You have answered rightly; do this and you will live." (Luke 10:25-28 NKJV)

The gospels include many examples of religious leaders being castigated by Jesus. But today we look at two readings which show religious experts exemplifying a proper understanding of faith. They struggled then, as we do now, with trying to understand how the message of Jesus Christ fits in with the message of the Hebrew Scriptures in which they were trained. In reading them, we see Jesus applauding their understanding that the new is bigger, greater, and more perfect than the old.

In seeing this, we return to the very first concept we examined: God is love. Jesus is the fulfillment of the law because Jesus is God, and God is love, and *love* is the law and the prophets.

Have you ever taken pride in your knowledge of the scriptures, and perhaps used that knowledge to condemn LGBTQ people, even in your own mind? Take heart and turn, like the scribe in Mark's gospel. There is still time for you to say along with him, that loving God and neighbor are more important than anything else.

When you do so, you will not be far from the kingdom of God.

Jesus must not be read as having baited us with grace only to clobber us in the end with law. For as the death and resurrection of Jesus were accomplished once and for all, so the grace that reigns by those mysteries reigns eternally – even in the thick of judgment.

Robert Farrar Capon

WHO DOES JESUS CONDEMN AND WHY?

Our previous readings have revealed that Jesus was quite a rebel, and radically inclusive. So did he chastise anyone? The answer is yes, and you'll see who those people were as we continue our study this week.

DAY 20: THOSE WHO SHUT THE DOOR OF HEAVEN

"Woe to you, teachers of the law and Pharisees, you hypocrites! You shut the door of the kingdom of heaven in people's faces." "And so upon you will come all the righteous blood that has been shed on earth"
(Matthew 23:13, 35 NIV)

Jesus was harsh to only two groups: those who turned his father's house into a marketplace, and the scribes and Pharisees, who blocked the way to the kingdom and bore their religiosity like a golden hammer.

Many Christians hold a Bible-alone theology, and believe the scriptures are evergreen in their entirety. Many of us think that all the rules presented in them still apply (except in the case of haircuts, fabric composition, stoning, and dozens of others we lump into "Old Covenant.")

But doing this dismisses Jesus' woes to the Pharisees we read in today's passage from Matthew 23, and deems them merely historical. We snicker about those persnickety Pharisees, who counted cumin seeds and nagged about tiny bugs in the meager wine cups of the poor. Many of us moderns feel good about what we believe is our own simpler relationship, based on faith, and seem to think if Jesus' woes apply to anyone, it's to the Roman Catholics.

But this is exactly the kind of viperish hypocrisy which Jesus condemned. From many pulpits we hear (or preach) that all of the scriptures continue to apply to Christians today: all the parables, all Paul's warnings about sin, and most especially those few mentions of same-sex relations.

But we don't seem to think Jesus' woes should be viewed as a warning to God's people today. And that seems exceedingly odd, given the unprecedented harshness of Jesus' stance, and the sheer force of his derisive disapproval.

Jesus never speaks to anyone in the scriptures that way again. It's to this group of rule-wielding "God defenders" alone that he unleashes the full force of his verbal condemnation. And this warning is evergreen.

He's still unleashing his disapproval on those who continue to do it today.

Let's strive to open our hearts to love, and try not to shut the door of heaven in the faces of our LGBTQ loved ones. None of us wants Jesus to speak to us the way he spoke woe to the ancient law-wielders.

Every time we use religion to draw a line to keep people out, Jesus is with the people on the other side of that line.
Hugh L. Hollowell

DAY 21: NEGLECTORS OF JUSTICE, MERCY, AND FAITH

"Woe to you, scribes and Pharisees, hypocrites! For you tithe mint, dill, and cummin, and have neglected the weightier matters of the law: justice and mercy and faith. It is these you ought to have practiced without neglecting the others. You blind guides! You strain out a gnat but swallow a camel!" (Matthew 23:23-24 NRSVCE)

We continue today with Jesus' proclamation of woe to the religious experts.

We often feel good about doing the lesser things: going to church, tithing, and praying before dinner. But today's words from Jesus aren't simply historical artifacts. They are intended to pierce our very souls. They should convict us to always strive for deeper faith, lived out more fully. He calls justice and mercy "weightier matters of the law," and that means for us as well as for those long-dead faith leaders.

It can be hard to shake Pharisaical thinking when it has been shaped and honed throughout our lives. We are quick to draw scripture passages as weapons, ready to cut off efforts to speak love and truth. And so we must return regularly to this verse. We must pray for revelation about what justice means for the same-sex couple who wants to celebrate God's bringing them together by marrying in church. Or what it means for the transgender youth who wants to use the bathroom with the other guys. Or what it means for the family of a transgender woman who worries she will be murdered in the street. We need to ask God what mercy looks like for these people, in these circumstances. And then we need to live out those actions of mercy in response.

When we do this, we can be sure that Jesus himself will be watching in approval, and cheering us on.

Jesus condemned no one except hypocrites.
Kallistos Ware

Day 22: Deniers of Access to God

Since the Passover of the Jews was near, Jesus went up to Jerusalem. He found in the temple area those who sold oxen, sheep, and doves, as well as the money-changers seated there. He made a whip out of cords and drove them all out of the temple area, with the sheep and oxen, and spilled the coins of the money-changers and overturned their tables, and to those who sold doves he said, "Take these out of here, and stop making my Father's house a marketplace." His disciples recalled the words of scripture, "Zeal for your house will consume me." (John 2:13-17 NABRE)

The second chapter of John's gospel opens with the wedding at Cana, showing us that Jesus' first miraculous action was purely a gift of love and joy: wine for the people gathered to celebrate a wedding. John then moves on to show us an angry Christ.

The money changers and animal purveyors were nothing new to Jesus. As devout Jews, his family would have dutifully traveled to Jerusalem each year for Passover. He knew the abusers of his Father's house would be there this year as well, and so he prepared by tying together cords to use as a whip. His fury was premeditated.

Some say he was just mad that people were making money in the temple. But Jesus has never been terribly concerned about money. What he *is* concerned about is people. In this scenario, year after year, people were earnestly trying to obey the law by offering sacrifices at Passover. Many traveled long distances to be there, wanting to meet God in his sanctuary. But those who changed money at a price and sold animals at inflated costs were a barrier. For some of the faithful, the cost they exacted was too high, and kept them from entering.

Many socially conservative Christians perform that same function today. When our LGBTQ brothers and sisters long to be obedient Christians by showing up at church to worship God, we ask them to deny their identities. To deny their very being.

Jesus brandished whips at those who exacted too high a price for access to God's house. He cannot be happy with those of us who continue to do so now.

We do not see Jesus condemning the sinners in the world; rather, he condemns the leaders of God's people with his severest words.
Jerram Barrs

Day 23: Those Who Will Not Produce Good Fruit

But when he saw many of the Pharisees and Sadducees coming to where he was baptizing, he said to them: "You brood of vipers! Who warned you to flee from the coming wrath? Produce fruit in keeping with repentance. And do not think you can say to yourselves, 'We have Abraham as our father.' I tell you that out of these stones God can raise up children for Abraham. The ax is already at the root of the trees, and every tree that does not produce good fruit will be cut down and thrown into the fire.
(Matthew 3:7-10 NIV)

From the earliest days of Jesus' ministry, the warnings rang out. In today's case the warning comes through the voice of John the Baptist. He calls the religious elite a "brood of vipers," which is a phrase Jesus echoed later. John tried to warn them they need to change their mode of thinking, because it wasn't what God wants. The Pharisees and Sadducees thought they had the path to righteousness all sewn up based on their study of the scriptures and theoretical adherence to the law. But they weren't producing good fruit:

But the fruit of the Spirit is love, joy, peace, forbearance, kindness, goodness, faithfulness, gentleness and self-control. (Galatians 5:22-23 NIV)

How much fruit are you producing, particularly as it relates to the LGBTQ loved ones in your life?

Some of the Pharisees and Sadducees listened to John's warning, and did indeed repent. Others continued to demand God was a harsh taskmaster who determined our eternal destinies based on how closely we followed the particular sets of rules and regulations they determined to be required. They didn't hear what John was trying to tell them. Perhaps they couldn't hear.

Matthew tells us God could raise up believers out of the very stones themselves. If he can do that, he most certainly can raise up children for Jesus from amongst the LGBTQ community. And he will most certainly revel in the fruit they bear.

> *The causes of my uneasiness are these: 1. The lack of spiritual fruit in the lives of so many who claim to have faith. 2. The rarity of a radical change in the conduct and general outlook of persons professing their new faith in Christ as their personal Saviour.....Plain horse sense ought to tell us that anything that makes no change in the man who professes it makes no difference to God either, and it is an easily observable fact that for countless numbers of persons the change from no-faith to faith makes no actual difference in the life.*
> A.W. Tozer

ABOUT YOUR LOVED ONE

Now that we've spent time thinking and praying about the things which act as the foundation of our faith, we can move on to topics which probably concern you about your LGBTQ loved one. Breathe deep, and ask that the Holy Spirit continue to carry you through this 50-day retreat.

All will be well.

CAN A SINNER BE CHRISTIAN?

Many of us are taught that once a person is saved, they no longer sin, and if they do sin, they weren't actually saved. But a variety of New Testament passages contradict this concept. Over the next few days we'll take a look at some of these verses so you can make up your own mind about the issue.

Day 24: Paul Calls Himself a Sinner

Here is a trustworthy saying that deserves full acceptance: Christ Jesus came into the world to save sinners—of whom I am the worst.
(1 Timothy 1:16 NIV)

I do not understand what I do. For what I want to do I do not do, but what I hate I do. And if I do what I do not want to do, I agree that the law is good. As it is, it is no longer I myself who do it, but it is sin living in me. For I know that good itself does not dwell in me, that is, in my sinful nature. For I have the desire to do what is good, but I cannot carry it out. For I do not do the good I want to do, but the evil I do not want to do—this I keep on doing. Now if I do what I do not want to do, it is no longer I who do it, but it is sin living in me that does it.

So I find this law at work: Although I want to do good, evil is right there with me. For in my inner being I delight in God's law; but I see another law at work in me, waging war against the law of my mind and making me a prisoner of the law of sin at work within me. What a wretched man I am! Who will rescue me from this body that is subject to death? Thanks be to God, who delivers me through Jesus Christ our Lord! (Romans 7:15-25 NIV)

St. Paul is an interesting person. He is the hero of many Christians who point to him when we want to decry the mote of dust in our brother's eye. We demand the passages in which Paul points out various sinful behaviors prove sinners don't make it to heaven. We ignore the logs in our own eyes. We also ignore this passage, in which Paul says that despite having an encounter with Christ which literally knocked him off his high horse, he remained a sinner.

Some try to say Paul put all of that sin stuff behind him, but these passages are clear. He says he kept on doing it.

Humans are sinners, and Christians are humans. But luckily we can all say the final line of today's reading along with Paul: *Thanks be to God, who delivers me through Jesus Christ our Lord!*

If my sinfulness appears to me to be in any way smaller or less detestable in comparison with the sins of others, I am still not recognizing my sinfulness at all. ... How can I possibly serve another person in unfeigned humility if I seriously regard his sinfulness as worse than my own?
Dietrich Bonhoeffer

47

DAY 25: JESUS PRAISES A WORSHIPPER OF MANY GODS

When Jesus had entered Capernaum, a centurion came to him, asking for help. "Lord," he said, "my servant lies at home paralyzed, suffering terribly." Jesus said to him, "Shall I come and heal him?" The centurion replied, "Lord, I do not deserve to have you come under my roof. But just say the word, and my servant will be healed. For I myself am a man under authority, with soldiers under me. I tell this one, 'Go,' and he goes; and that one, 'Come,' and he comes. I say to my servant, 'Do this,' and he does it." When Jesus heard this, he was amazed and said to those following him, "Truly I tell you, I have not found anyone in Israel with such great faith. I say to you that many will come from the east and the west, and will take their places at the feast with Abraham, Isaac and Jacob in the kingdom of heaven." (Matthew 8:5-11 NIV)

Centurions were officers in the Roman military who commanded groups of soldiers called "legionaries." Responsibilities included training, assigning work details, and administering discipline. They were paid much more than a normal soldier, and were powerful and highly respected. However, they were Romans, and Romans were polytheistic, meaning they worshipped multiple gods.

The Ten Commandments and nearly all the books of the Bible contain warnings about idolatry. Hundreds of passages describe God's wrath against idolaters. In the epistles, Paul repeatedly warns against slipping back into the ways of those who worship the old gods. Given his military responsibilities, the centurion in this passage was probably a devotee of Mars, the god of war. From a polytheistic viewpoint, he would have had no problem adding a new entity into his personal pantheon. He heard of Jesus and believed. He acknowledged that Jesus' power was so great he could simply speak a command of deliverance and healing, and the servant would be freed, from miles away.

The centurion was undoubtedly an idolatrous sinner of the kind decried throughout scriptures, and yet look at Jesus' amazed words. He says he had not found such faith among the "faithful" of Israel.

He said many like that idolater would participate in the heavenly feast.

We will all be wrong about many things in our lifetime. We will sin. But God doesn't expect perfection. He desires our yearning for his will, and for love, and for faith.

The sinners to whom Jesus directed His messianic ministry were not those who skipped morning devotions or Sunday church. His ministry was to those whom society considered real sinners. They had done nothing to merit salvation. Yet they opened themselves to the gift that was offered them. On the other hand, the self-righteous placed their trust in the works of the Law and closed their hearts to the message of grace.
Brennan Manning

Day 26: Tax Collectors and Prostitutes Enter Heaven

Jesus entered the temple courts, and, while he was teaching, the chief priests and the elders of the people came to him. "By what authority are you doing these things?" they asked. "And who gave you this authority?"
Jesus said to them, "Truly I tell you, the tax collectors and the prostitutes are entering the kingdom of God ahead of you. For John came to you to show you the way of righteousness, and you did not believe him, but the tax collectors and the prostitutes did. And even after you saw this, you did not repent and believe him. (Matthew 21:23, 31-32 NIV)

The religious authorities of Jesus' day walked in pride, believing they knew all about what God wanted and how to make him happy. A great percentage of the gospels are Jesus' tireless attempts to get them to realize they were wrong. Today's passage is one more example.

Jesus mentions two groups of despised people—prostitutes and tax collectors—to try to rattle the chief priests and elders off their high and mighty perches. By their rules, prostitutes and tax collectors should *never* make it to heaven.

And yet Jesus' response is clear: the rules had changed. Love and mercy were the new commandments which overrode all others. Those who believed that truth, regardless of their lot in life or their standing within the religious community, were entering the kingdom of God.

They continue to do so today.

How weary God must be when we echo those chief priests and elders of old, continuing to demand our righteousness, and denying that Love is truly the answer?

Nothing that we despise in other men is inherently absent from ourselves. We must learn to regard people less in the light of what they do or don't do, and more in light of what they suffer.
Dietrich Bonhoeffer

Day 27: If We Claim to Be Without Sin We Deceive Ourselves

For we have already made the charge that Jews and Gentiles alike are all under the power of sin. As it is written: "There is no one righteous, not even one" (Romans 3:9-10 NIV)

For there is no distinction, since all have sinned and fall short of the glory of God; they are now justified by his grace as a gift, through the redemption that is in Christ Jesus, whom God put forward as a sacrifice of atonement by his blood, effective through faith.
(Romans 3:22-25 NRSV)

If we claim to be without sin, we deceive ourselves and the truth is not in us. If we confess our sins, he is faithful and just and will forgive us our sins and purify us from all unrighteousness. If we claim we have not sinned, we make him out to be a liar and his word is not in us.
*(*1 John 1:8-10 NIV)

Today is our last day of examining whether or not Christians can be sinners. We end it like a fireworks display, with multiple pops and bangs firing at once, though in this case, the rockets are scripture passages.

The first thing to remember is that the epistles weren't written to non-believers who the authors would *expect* to sin. They are addressed to the leaders of various churches; the experts in Christianity at the time. And apparently those leaders needed correction in their understanding of this very issue, because both John and Paul felt the need to make it clear we are *all* sinners. Paul points out that in fact, there are no distinctions. He is trying to get the church in Rome to stop making distinctions because the reality of our nature is singular.

But John's words should rattle the bones of us modern day Christians who demand LGBTQ persons can't be Christian because of their supposed sinfulness. If we try to claim Christians are not sinners, John says we are making Jesus out to be a liar, and his word is not in us.

We all fall, and we are all justified through the miraculous gift of Jesus. Pretending otherwise is a slap in the face of the Christ.

> *Now I wonder whether I have sufficiently realized that during all this time God has been trying to find me, to know me, and to love me. The question is not "How am I to find God?" but "How am I to let myself be found by him?" The question is not "How am I to know God?" but "How am I to let myself be known by God?" And, finally, the question is not "How am I to love God?" but "How am I to let myself be loved by God?" God is looking into the distance for me, trying to find me, and longing to bring me home.*
> Henri J.M. Nouwen

MALE AND FEMALE, GOD CREATED THEM

It's time. We've reached the topics which make many of us extremely uncomfortable: gender and sexuality. But there's nothing to be afraid of.

To kick off this area of focus, we examine the mystery of male and female through the lens of scripture.

DAY 28: MALE AND FEMALE HE CREATED THEM

Then God said, "Let us make mankind in our image, in our likeness, so that they may rule over the fish in the sea and the birds in the sky, over the livestock and all the wild animals, and over all the creatures that move along the ground." So God created mankind in his own image, in the image of God he created them; male and female he created them.
(Genesis 1:26-27 NIV)

Most of us miss the full import of this passage. We focus on the binary and read it as God having made us male OR female. But the statement is so much more profound than that, because it speaks not only about human gender identity, but about God himself. And that's a biggie.

Read the passage again, but slow down this time, and focus on the last sentence:

So God created mankind in his own image, in the image of God he created them; male and female he created them.

Did you catch it in this reading? In the image of God he created them, male AND female. It doesn't say "or," it says "and," which tells us *God* is both, and we are not binary.

This may seem like verbal gymnastics, but it truly isn't. Many of us tout the passage as the definitive indictment of non-conforming gender and sexual identities. We demand that LGBTQ people take the words to mean what they say. Because of this, it's only logical that we should examine the words closely, and delve deep into the awesome mystery of God's creation, and of his very being.

The majority of our adult population grew up with traditional concepts of femininity and masculinity, and associates gender with sex characteristics. Many schools of Christian thought believe we carry a binary gender when we leave our bodies. But when we are no longer equipped with genitalia, Adam's apples, or bone structure, what will our gender resemble? Will our presences in the mystical state known as heaven be intensified versions of binary genders, or will our spirits broaden to be even more like God? More fully *both*, just as God is?

When we allow the Holy Spirit to breathe meaning through today's scripture we make a magnificent discovery:

We are made in the male and female image of God. This means that gender fluid people are actually more God-like than those who identify with a gender binary.

> *Deep inside the universe lies the potential of the phenomena of consciousness. The mystery of "you" existed as a potential within the stuff of matter for billions of years, and before that within the infinite sea of consciousness that is God, of which you are a wave. Here you are, birthed out of the ecstatic merging of two others, you are consciousness that learns and grows. You are a child of the universe, a child of the stars, a child of the earth, a child of God, blossomed from love into an infinite love awakening. In all infinite time and possibilities, infinity gave way to you.*
> *Here you are.*
> Jacob. M. Wright

DAY 29: GENDER IDENTIFICATION IN THE TALMUD

When God created mankind, he made them in the likeness of God. He created them male and female and blessed them.
(Genesis 5:1-2 NIV)

Today we look to the Jewish roots of our faith. The Talmud is an ancient collection of 63 tractates which instructed Jews on how to live. One of the tractates talks about the intersection of biological sex and gender performance, and lists these four categories in addition to male and female:

Androgynos: a person whose external sex characteristics are both male and female.

Tumtum: a person whose external sex characteristics are hidden or unclear.

Aylonit: a biological female who hasn't started to look "womanly" by the time she is 20.

Saris: a biological male who hasn't started to look "manly" by the time he is 20.

These descriptions are driven by body parts rather than identity. The system was developed because gender rules for behavior were closely connected to whether a person was biologically male or female. The Old Testament is filled with rules for male and female behavior.

Here's one example for how gender assignment played out:

Blowing a shofar and listening to the sound was an important part of some religious rituals. Males were allowed to blow it for everyone to hear. Androgynos could blow it only for other androgynos to hear. Tumtum could blow it only for themselves to hear.

As with Christianity, most of these rules are no longer followed by Jewish congregations. But at the time of writing, the Jewish faithful recognized that biological sex and gender were non-binary and had to find a way for non-binary people to know what they could and couldn't do. Judaism is the religion out of which Christianity sprang. It held rules and law to be intrinsically connected to righteousness, yet understood the reality of sex and gender variety. Isn't it odd that so many of us Christians today can't accept that reality?

> *The more we let God take us over, the more truly ourselves we become —*
> *because He made us. He invented us. He invented all the different people*
> *that you and I were intended to be.*
> C.S. Lewis

DAY 30: THE EUNUCH WHO DESIRES BAPTISM

Now an angel of the Lord said to Philip, "Rise and go toward the south
to the road that goes down from Jerusalem to Gaza." This is a desert
place. And he rose and went. And there was an Ethiopian, a eunuch, a
court official of Candace, queen of the Ethiopians, who was in charge of all
her treasure. He had come to Jerusalem to worship and was returning,
seated in his chariot, and he was reading the prophet Isaiah. And the
Spirit said to Philip, "Go over and join this chariot." So Philip ran to
him and heard him reading Isaiah the prophet and asked, "Do you
understand what you are reading?" And he said, "How can I, unless
someone guides me?" And he invited Philip to come up and sit with him.
Then Philip opened his mouth, and beginning with this Scripture he told
him the good news about Jesus. And as they were going along the road they
came to some water, and the eunuch said, "See, here is water! What
prevents me from being baptized?" And he commanded the chariot to stop,
and they both went down into the water, Philip and the eunuch, and he
baptized him. And when they came up out of the water, the Spirit of the
Lord carried Philip away, and the eunuch saw him no more, and went on
his way rejoicing.
(Acts 8:26-31, 35-39 ESV)

What an exciting tale this is! The imagery is vivid: an Ethiopian person studies scripture while riding in a royal chariot, the way we might read a novel on a long drive. Owning scrolls of scripture was no small thing, and it can't have been easy reading given the bumps of wooden or iron-clad wheels across cobbled streets and mud ruts. Phillip must have been quite surprised by what he found when he followed the Spirit's instructions to join them.

Despite his lofty position within the queen's court, the eunuch demonstrates humility in admitting he can't truly understand the words of Isaiah. And when Phillip tells the good news, he is quick to respond, requesting baptism so he could embrace this new thing Jesus promised.

Phillip baptizes the eunuch as requested. He could find no reason not to baptize him, despite his non-binary status.

Once the baptism is complete, Phillip is carried away by the Spirit (which must have blown the eunuch's mind).

The eunuch surely carried his excitement back to Ethiopia, sharing the gospel message and explaining what he'd experienced; becoming an exuberant, non-binary evangelist.

It seems odd that despite the power of this passage and the important role the Ethiopian held within his country's royal court, the eunuch remains unnamed. But perhaps the lack of a name is a good thing, because it means that all LGBTQ people can put themselves in the place of this non-binary person who hungers for God, and for whom Philip can find no reason to refuse baptism.

There have always been transgender and gender non-conforming people. There will always be trans and gender non-conforming people. Trans and gender non-conforming people turn up in every culture and every population. In fact, the first gentile Christian in the Book of Acts was someone who could be viewed as gender non-conforming—the Ethiopian Eunuch.
Vivian Taylor

DAY 31: DEUTERONOMY ON CROSS-DRESSING

A woman shall not wear a man's garment, nor shall a man put on a woman's cloak, for whoever does these things is an abomination to the Lord your God.
(Deuteronomy 22:5 ESV)

At the time of Deuteronomy's writing, cultic temple worship included cross-dressing. Men wearing colorful female clothing could be found in the temples of Astarte, Ashtaroth, or Venus, and armor-clad women could be found worshipping Mars.

The Hebrew Scriptures are saturated with the problems and pitfalls of turning away from Yahweh, so it's logical that instructions for faithful Jewish life would include warnings against cross-dressing because of its cultural connection to idolatry.

Inclusion of the term "abomination" underscores the connection to idol worship. If you check a concordance for the term and review the list of verses which include it, you will quickly see its intrinsic coupling with the worship of other gods.

In other words, the author of Deuteronomy probably wasn't concerned about which robe was for females, and which was for males. (After all, everyone wore dresses). The author was concerned about faithfulness and not misleading others into thinking they were turning away from God.

Even if this wasn't the case, let's look at a few more instructions about clothing from the same chapter:

You shall not wear cloth of wool and linen mixed together. "You shall make yourself tassels on the four corners of the garment with which you cover yourself. (Deuteronomy 22:11-12 ESV)

How many of the Christians you know actually check the fabric content of their clothing so that they don't offend God? Do you? How many Christians do you see sporting tassels on their coats? Does your coat have them?

It's hypocritical to say that one set of injunctions about dress should be adhered to strictly while completely disregarding additional instructions which appear just six verses later. Let's not be spiritual hypocrites.

If Jesus came to bring abundant life to all who follow him, that means that transgender Christians should be able to stop spending every single bit of their energy defending themselves against those 'clobber passages,' in order to concentrate instead on becoming better disciples. We should be able to move from survival practices to thriving faith. Jesus didn't come to make things marginally more bearable. He came to give us abundant and eternal life.

Austen Hartke

DAY 32: FEARFULLY AND WONDERFULLY MADE

Where can I go from your Spirit? Where can I flee from your presence? If I go up to the heavens, you are there; if I make my bed in the depths, you are there. If I rise on the wings of the dawn, if I settle on the far side of the sea, even there your hand will guide me, your right hand will hold me fast. If I say, "Surely the darkness will hide me and the light become night around me," even the darkness will not be dark to you; the night will shine like the day, for darkness is as light to you. For you created my inmost being; knit me together in my mother's womb. I praise you because I am fearfully and wonderfully made; your works are wonderful, I know that full well. My frame was not hidden from you when I was made in the secret place, I was woven together in the depths of the earth. Your eyes saw my unformed body; all the days ordained for me were written in your book before one of them came to be. (Psalm 139:7-16 NIV)

LGBTQ individuals face a lot of criticism about key issues of identity. Gay, lesbian, and bisexual people just want to be able to love who they love and are attracted to. Transgender people just want to live life according to their true gender. Conservative Christians talk about these things as if they are choices and decisions.

But they aren't.

And you know what? God knows it, even if we don't. He knows it because he formed each of us in our mothers' wombs. As Christians we believe God is in charge of our existence from the very beginning. As Christians we know God doesn't make mistakes. LGBTQ individuals were formed uniquely and particularly, with all their strengths, weaknesses, inherent skills and talents, physical attributes, and brain power. Just like everyone else. We can take no credit in the fact that we are fast runners, have pretty eyes, are good at math, or have straight teeth. These are all gifts from the God who formed us in the womb. We also can take no credit for our gender or our sexuality, nor can we be condemned for them.

We didn't choose them. God did.

Know that your LGBTQ loved ones are fearfully and wonderfully made, just as they are. They can't hide who they are from God, nor do they need to. He doesn't want them to. He is holding them even while you struggle with your worry and confusion, and all their days are written in his book.

God did not create a black and white world of male and female. Creation is not black and white, it is amazingly diverse, like a rainbow, including sexualities and a variety of non-heterosexual expressions of behaviour, affection and partnering occurring in most species, including humans.
Anthony Venn-Brown

DAY 33: GOD'S PROMISE TO NON-BINARY BELIEVERS

This is what the Lord says: "Maintain justice and do what is right, for my salvation is close at hand and my righteousness will soon be revealed. Blessed is the one who does this—the person who holds it fast, who keeps the Sabbath without desecrating it, and keeps their hands from doing any evil." Let no foreigner who is bound to the Lord say, "The Lord will surely exclude me from his people." And let no eunuch complain, "I am only a dry tree." For this is what the Lord says: "To the eunuchs who keep my Sabbaths, who choose what pleases me and hold fast to my covenant—to them I will give within my temple and its walls a memorial and a name better than sons and daughters; I will give them an everlasting name that will endure forever.
(Isaiah 56:1-5, NIV)

Christians frequently quote the prophet Isaiah's calls for repentance and predictions of the Messiah to come. But Isaiah also speaks about what things will be like in the future days of restoration and glory.

We can see from today's passage that foreigners and eunuchs may not have felt the same hope those we call the "chosen people" did. There was obviously fear that being "other" would exclude them from God's promises, simply due to that otherness.

But the passage continues on to show us God's response to this thinking. We read about the call for justice, for relationship with God, and for fighting against our internal desires toward selfishness. We also read about the reward to non-binary people who strive for these things. To these people, God promises not merely a place at God's table, but a name "better than sons and daughters." A special place, and a special reward, above that given to those who may believe they have more right to God's blessing.

So let's all strive for what pleases God, and hold fast to the promises of Jesus Christ. In doing so, like the eunuchs, we are given an everlasting name which endures forever.

A name which means "beloved."

Every creature is a divine word because it proclaims God.
St. Bonaventure

SEXUALITY AND MARRIAGE

Marriages are imploding all around us. Sometimes you can see it coming years ahead of time. Other times it is a surprise. Meanwhile, our Christian focus seems to be on the idea that the destruction of family is coming about through gay marriage.

In this section we'll explore the Bible's presentation of sexuality and marriage to discover God's vision of loving marital unity.

May your hearts and minds be opened by the Holy Spirit to receive what he would speak to you.

DAY 34: ADAM AND EVE ARE NOT THE OPTIMAL MODEL FOR MARRIAGE

The Lord God said, "It is not good for the man to be alone. I will make a helper suitable for him." So the Lord God caused the man to fall into a deep sleep; and while he was sleeping, he took one of the man's ribs and then closed up the place with flesh. Then the Lord God made a woman from the rib he had taken out of the man, and he brought her to the man.
(Genesis 2:18, 21-22 NIV)

One of the primary Christian arguments against same sex marriage is the Genesis account of human creation. "It was Adam and Eve, not Adam and Steve!" is a frequent refrain. But can that pair *really* be God's image of an ideal marriage?

The first problem with this notion is that Eve seems to be the inauguration of human cloning (though God added a tail to the Y chromosome in the process). Most people agree that mating with our closest genetic match isn't such a great idea, and a number of scriptures decry it. The second problem is that Adam and Eve were the only humans available. They had no one else to pick; it was just them, the animals, and that wicked serpent. In Western cultures, most people believe we should have a say about whom we choose to marry, but Adam and Eve had no choice. The third problem is the pair was immediately dysfunctional. They didn't communicate when temptation arose, Adam blamed Eve for their joint mistake, and just look at what happened to their kids! Lastly, this first couple, who are at the heart of the one-man-one-woman argument, never had what we consider marriage today. Their union may have been sanctioned by God, but it certainly wasn't officiated over by either church or state.

So let's put the whole thing together. If Adam and Eve *are* the optimal model for marriage, we Christians must conclude the following:

Marriage should be between genetic twins, should not involve choice of partner, should not require civil or ecclesiastic involvement, and should be dysfunctional.

This sounds like a list of everything a marriage should *not* be! But that's okay, because Adam and Eve were never meant to provide a paradigm for marriage. The salvation story as a whole is the model for coupling, culminating in the sacrificial love of Christ. The prototype for marriage centers on fidelity, trust, love, covenant, forgiveness, and generosity. None of those things are demonstrated in the Adam and Eve accounts in Genesis.

Surely Adam and Steve could do better.

From a theological perspective, marriage primarily involves a covenant-keeping relationship of mutual self-giving that reflects God's love for us.
Matthew Vines

DAY 35: "TRADITIONAL" MARRIAGE

This is a faithful saying: If a man desires the position of a bishop, he desires a good work. A bishop then must be blameless, the husband of one wife, temperate, sober-minded, of good behavior, hospitable, able to teach; not given to wine, not violent, not greedy for money, but gentle, not quarrelsome, not covetous; one who rules his own house well, having his children in submission with all reverence (for if a man does not know how to rule his own house, how will he take care of the church of God?); not a novice, lest being puffed up with pride he fall into the same condemnation as the devil. (1 Timothy 3:1-6 NKJV)

Socially conservative Christians demand that the Bible says marriage is between one man and one woman, calling this "traditional marriage." But what does "traditional" mean? Most often the word is related to time; the length of a practice and its repetition renders something a tradition. So let's look at the "one man, one woman/traditional marriage" argument from the perspective of time.

Polygynous marriage (one man, more than one woman) was alive and well in Christianity until relatively recently. As you can see from today's passage, it was thriving in the young Christian community, enough so that Paul counseled Bishops to have only *one* wife. This makes it clear polygyny was okay for everyone else: priests, deacons, and lay people. He didn't condemn having multiple wives in this letter, nor did he in any of the others.

The years marched on, and two doctors of the church—St. Augustine and St. Basil of Caesarea—also wrote about the practice without condemnation in the 4th century. Socrates of Constantinople addressed it in the 5th. In the 16th century, Reformation hero Martin Luther proclaimed it permissible under some circumstances, saying:

I confess that I cannot forbid a person to marry several wives, for it does not contradict the Scripture. If a man wishes to marry more than one wife he should be asked whether he is satisfied in his conscience that he may do so in accordance with the word of God. In such a case the civil authority has nothing to do in the matter.

The Council of Trent took a firm stance on the issue in 1563, finally declaring polygyny and concubinage anathema. We'll ignore the polygyny which continues in some Mormon circles and call 1563 the beginning of "one man, one woman." It's been 455 years since then (as of the date of this writing).

Abraham is the first biblical example of polygyny, and he walked the earth around 2,000BCE. That means for at least 3,560+ years, marriage between one man and more than one woman was common among the faithful. That's 3,560+ years of polygyny compared to 455 years of "one man, one woman".

Which, then, is more "traditional?"

The marriage institution cannot exist among slaves, and one sixth of the population of democratic America is denied its privileges by the law of the land. What is to be thought of a nation boasting of its liberty, boasting of its humanity, boasting of its Christianity, boasting of its love of justice and purity, and yet having within its own borders three millions of persons denied by law the right of marriage?
Frederick Douglass

DAY 36: LET MARRIAGE BE HELD IN HONOR

*Let marriage be held in honor by all, and let the marriage bed be kept
undefiled; for God will judge fornicators and adulterers.*
(Hebrews 13:4 NRSV)

Marriage is a sacred union which weaves two souls into a cord of
three strands with God. When God draws couples together into this
sacred union, no one should try to separate them, as scripture tells us.

Unfortunately, not all marriages are orchestrated by God. Not all of
them are holy. Let's look at it in concrete terms. Of the two scenarios
below, which would the Christian God of love prefer? Which better
represents God's desire for holy union?

A heterosexual couple who was forced into marriage by their
parents due to unplanned pregnancy, and who treats each other with
disdain, lies, cheats, and dishonors one another, hides what little light
they permit to shine under a bushel, and shows the world marriage is
a bitter pill to swallow.

or

A same sex couple who treats each other with respect, lives life
together joyfully, mutually commits to truth and fidelity, studies
God's word together, worships together, serves their church together,
and acts as bearers of light and life, and carriers of the good news.

Obviously not all heterosexual couples fit the first profile, nor all
same-sex couples the second. Both types of marriages can be found
in both scenarios. But of these two, which holds marriage in honor?
Of which type is Jesus more likely to say "Well done?"

*Marriage, in its truest sense, is a partnership of equals, with neither
exercising dominion over the other, but, rather, with each encouraging and
assisting the other in whatever responsibilities and aspirations he or she
might have.*
Gordon B. Hinckley

DAY 37: ISAIAH AND EZEKIEL ON SODOM AND GOMORRAH

Hear the word of the Lord, you rulers of Sodom; listen to the instruction of our God, you people of Gomorrah! "The multitude of your sacrifices—what are they to me?" says the Lord. "I have more than enough of burnt offerings, of rams and the fat of fattened animals; I have no pleasure in the blood of bulls and lambs and goats. Stop bringing meaningless offerings! Your incense is detestable to me. When you spread out your hands in prayer, I hide my eyes from you; even when you offer many prayers, I am not listening. Your hands are full of blood! Wash and make yourselves clean. Take your evil deeds out of my sight; stop doing wrong. Learn to do right; seek justice. Defend the oppressed. Take up the cause of the fatherless; plead the case of the widow. "Come now, let us settle the matter," says the Lord. "Though your sins are like scarlet, they shall be as white as snow; though they are red as crimson, they shall be like wool. If you are willing and obedient, you will eat the good things of the land; but if you resist and rebel, you will be devoured by the sword." For the mouth of the Lord has spoken. (Isaiah 1:10-11, 13, 15-20 NIV)

"Now this was the sin of your sister Sodom: She and her daughters were arrogant, overfed and unconcerned; they did not help the poor and needy." (Ezekiel 16:49 NIV)

Sodom and Gomorrah are used more than any other Bible story to admonish people about same-sex relationships. The fact that a crowd of men pounded on Lot's door and demanded to rape the visiting angels has become the rallying cry for why men should not love men, and women should not love women.

But this interpretation has a lot of flaws. If this was a town in which homosexual behavior was so pervasive, why would the men need to come en masse to have sex with the angels? A town full of people doesn't suddenly become so sexually aroused they are overcome and need an outlet. If that was the case, they would simply turn to each other to fulfill their desire.

The answer is they weren't there to have run-of-the-mill sex with the angels they believed to be men. They were there to *rape* them.

Rape was an action of violence and power and remains so today. At that time, rape was a sign of victory over an opponent. In this case, it appears the men of the town wished to display their victory over the desires of God for love, mercy, and hospitality. You can almost imagine the demonic horde arriving to face off against the two angels of light, their faces distorted in gleeful anticipation and false triumph.

So if homosexuality wasn't at the root of the story, why did God display his wrath that violently?

Today's readings show us what two of the major prophets had to say about it. The first comes from Isaiah, harbinger of Jesus and remonstrator of the perpetually unfaithful followers of God. The prophet of prophets one might even say. What does Isaiah tells us about Sodom and Gomorrah? Does he talk about sexual behavior? No. Not even once. Isaiah warns us not to be like the people of those cities because they did not seek justice, defend the oppressed, care for the fatherless, and help the widow. He says it doesn't matter how closely we adhere to the law with all its rules about sacrifice and prayer, if we aren't doing justice. Ezekiel chimes in with the same message.

As Christians today, we can perform all sorts of pious practices which replaced the burning fat of rams from Isaiah's day. We can memorize Bible passages, tithe, and preach on street corners until our throats are sore. But without mercy and justice, we are like Isaiah's audience, which the Lord compares to the sinners of Sodom and Gomorrah.

Maybe [Sodom and Gomorrah] isn't really about homosexuality, but about rape. If the angels had been female, and the men of Sodom said they wanted to 'know' them against their will, would people claim that the story shows heterosexuality is a sin?
Alex Sanchez

WHAT DOES IT TAKE TO GET TO HEAVEN?

As we near the end of this devotional, we examine a few key verses about what it takes to be saved. The Bible's descriptions for this issue are many, varied, and often contradictory, which is why we *must* rely on the loving acceptance of the One who is love and mercy itself.

DAY 38: FOR GOD SO LOVED THE WORLD

For God so loved the world, that he gave his only Son, that whoever believes in him should not perish but have eternal life. (John 3:16 ESV)

We begin our meditations on the requirements for salvation with these electrifying words from the beloved disciple. Perhaps you've heard them so often they've come to sound trite or meaningless. But we start here because this single sentence contains the whole of the Good News: "…whoever believes in him should not perish but have eternal life."

"Whoever" is not qualified in any way. It doesn't say "whoever loves him but is without sin," or "whoever loves him and tithes 10%," or "whoever loves him and is heterosexual and cisgender." The term "whoever" stands alone.

Let's also look at the sentences which follow this verse:

For God did not send his Son into the world to condemn the world, but in order that the world might be saved through him. Whoever believes in him is not condemned.

Jesus addresses these statements to Nicodemus, who is referred to as a ruler of the Jews. Nicodemus came to question Jesus about how a person could be born again. Jesus chastises him because as a teacher of Israel, Nicodemus *should* have been able to understand. But he could not, or would not.

Nicodemus is a prefigurement of many of us today who have similar trouble.

John summarizes things for us so beautifully. First he says "In the beginning was the Word, and the Word was with God, and the Word was God." Then he tells us "For God so loved the world that he gave his only Son, that *whoever* believes in him should not perish but have eternal life."

Simple. Powerful. Inclusive. True.

Jesus Christ came not to condemn you but to save you, knowing your name, knowing all about you, knowing your weight right now, knowing your age, knowing what you do, knowing where you live, knowing what you ate for supper and what you will eat for breakfast, where you will sleep tonight, how much your clothing cost, who your parents were. He knows you individually as though there were not another person in the entire world. He died for you as certainly as if you had been the only lost one. He knows the worst about you and is the One who loves you the most.
A.W. Tozer

DAY 39: EVALUATION BY THE JUST JUDGE

Very truly I tell you, a time is coming and has now come when the dead will hear the voice of the Son of God and those who hear will live. For as the Father has life in himself, so he has granted the Son also to have life in himself. And he has given him authority to judge because he is the Son of Man.

"Do not be amazed at this, for a time is coming when all who are in their graves will hear his voice and come out—those who have done what is good will rise to live, and those who have done what is evil will rise to be condemned. By myself I can do nothing; I judge only as I hear, and my judgment is just, for I seek not to please myself but him who sent me.
(John 5:25-30 NIV)

The idea of judgement can be very scary for conservative Christians who have LGBTQ loved ones. So let's take a look at what the term "judgment" means.

A judge hears the facts of the case as presented by the accuser and the defendant, and then evaluates the evidence. Judging requires evaluation. At the time of our judgment, our lives will be evaluated. Our motives, our sorrows, our pressing needs, our weaknesses; all the messy mix of good and evil which make up the length of our years.

God's judgement is not binary, like an on/off switch in which you say the sinner's prayer and are in, or make love to someone of the same sex and are out. Binary issues don't require judgment. But over and over again the scriptures speak to us of judgment. And that requires analysis and a deep understanding of each situation.

Your LGBTQ loved one has Jesus as their judge. They don't have a particular verse in the Bible as their judge, or even the whole collection of books which make it up. They have a person, who is Love. He alone is their judge and yours, and he does actual judging.

And it is the Lord, it is Jesus, Who is my judge. Therefore I will try always to think leniently of others, that He may judge me leniently, or rather not at all, since He says: "Judge not, and ye shall not be judged."
Thérèse de Lisieux

78

Day 40: Righteousness through Faith

For the promise to Abraham or to his descendants that he would be heir of the world was not through the Law, but through the righteousness of faith. For if those who are of the Law are heirs, faith is made void and the promise is nullified; for the Law brings about wrath, but where there is no law, there also is no violation. In hope against hope he believed, so that he might become a father of many nations according to that which had been spoken, "So shall your descendants be." Therefore it was also credited to him as righteousness. (Romans 4:13-15, 18, 22 NASB)

Abraham is the father of Christianity, as well as that of Judaism and Islam. When the story described in today's passage took place, Abraham was elderly yet believed God's promise that his offspring would be as numerous as the stars in heaven or the sands of the seashore.

The essential reality of Christ's coming is summed up in today's passage. Our relationship with God is not through the law. After the exodus, Moses instituted a rigid structure of edicts and rules. From then on, the faithful believed our connection with God could only be maintained through elaborate and strict adherence to them. But here we have Abraham being held up as the epitome of righteousness; not because he performed the proper sacramental actions, and not because he was sinless. Scripture shows us he was just as flawed as we are. But his deep, abiding faith in God's promises is what counted.

His *faith* was credited to him as righteousness.

Our righteousness does not come through slavish adherence to law, nor to some impossible ideal of sinlessness. The same is true of your LGBTQ loved ones. Our righteousness and theirs, like Abraham's, comes only through faith.

Faith means the fundamental response to the love that has offered itself up for me. It thus becomes clear that faith is ordered primarily to the inconceivability of God's love, which surpasses us and anticipates us. Love alone is credible; nothing else can be believed, and nothing else ought to be believed. This is the achievement, the 'work' of faith: to recognize this absolute prius, which nothing else can surpass; to believe that there is such a thing as love, absolute love, and that there is nothing higher or greater than it.

Fr. Hans Urs Von Balthasar

Now it's Your Turn

We've walked together through an exploration of God, the Bible, Law, the reality of sinfulness, sexuality and gender, and requirements for heaven. Hopefully this has given you some degree of peace about your loved one.

Now it's time to look at yourself. What does God want you to do in response?

WHAT SHOULD YOU DO?

It's not a mistake that the LGBTQ person you love is in your life. Your response to them is a holy calling, and an opportunity for following more closely in the footsteps of Christ. Over the next few days we'll look at how you can cooperate with this call.

Day 41: Don't Turn Your Child Away from God

If one curses his father or his mother, his lamp will be put out in utter darkness. (Proverbs 20:20 RSV)

The eye that mocks a father
And scorns a mother,
The ravens of the valley will pick it out,
And the young eagles will eat it. (Proverbs 301:17 NASB)

Today's passages are admittedly not very uplifting. We may be tempted to repeat them to our LGBTQ kids as proof they need to mend their sinful ways.

But perhaps we should flip this idea around, and look in the mirror for a moment. Let's hear Paul on the subject:

Fathers, do not embitter your children, or they will become discouraged. (Colossians 3:21 NIV)

There's a reason the great apostle warns us not to discourage our children. By screaming at them about their sexual orientation or gender identity, we may make them turn away from God completely. They may not be able to reconcile the idea of a loving God with the Christianity you demonstrate. Your efforts to convince them of their sinfulness could mean they end up in utter darkness, or in the valley with birds of prey pecking away at their souls.

We know it is good, right, and proper for children to respect their parents; to listen to them and honor the roles they hold. But passages about what happens to those who do not should be a warning to parents as well. Your job is to protect your children, and to avoid making them bitter and discouraged. Your job is to love them, and to offer them acceptance and hope.

Leave the judging to Jesus, and encourage them to seek shelter in your protection, in an affirming church home, and in God.

Each day of our lives we make deposits in the memory banks of our children.
Charles R. Swindoll

Day 42: Love them Anyway

Then Jesus' mother and brothers arrived. Standing outside, they sent someone in to call him. A crowd was sitting around him, and they told him, "Your mother and brothers are outside looking for you." "Who are my mother and my brothers?" he asked. Then he looked at those seated in a circle around him and said, "Here are my mother and my brothers! Whoever does God's will is my brother and sister and mother."
(Mark 3:31-35 NIV)

Mary must have been pretty freaked out by this point. Her beloved son was traveling the countryside, violating laws, angering the religious experts, and hanging out with people society found undesirable.

Put yourself in her shoes. She watched her son doing all sorts of things which she thought put him in danger. She arrived at this time to try to protect her son, but he rejects her attempts at protection. She probably assumed she knew what was best for Jesus. After all; she was his mother. She probably had thoughts like "Can you please just not be so flamboyant," hoping he could hide who he was for even just a little bit longer so he'd be safe.

But we don't see her complaining in response to Jesus' words. She supported him despite being scared about what might happen.

One reason is that she knew who he was, down inside. Just like you know the son, daughter, sibling, or friend who's come out as gay or gender non-binary.

Obviously your LGBTQ loved one is not Jesus. None of us are. But we can still learn from Mary's response. She didn't try to stop him from living fully into who God the Father created him to be. She may not have understood it all, but she didn't have to. All she had to do was love Jesus and support him in the ways she could.

That's all you have to do as well. It may be impossible for you to understand how your loved one feels, or the decisions they make about how to live their life. But you don't have to. All you have to do is extend your love to them. God will cover the rest, and it's quite possible that it will be more beautiful than you could ever have imagined.

Just as it was for Mary.

You don't choose your family. They are God's gift to you, as you are to them.
Desmond Tutu

Day 43: Seek Unity

I ask not only on behalf of these, but also on behalf of those who will believe in me through their word, that they may all be one. As you, Father, are in me and I am in you, may they also be in us, so that the world may believe that you have sent me. The glory that you have given me I have given them, so that they may be one, as we are one, I in them and you in me, that they may become completely one, so that the world may know that you have sent me and have loved them even as you have loved me. Father, I desire that those also, whom you have given me, may be with me where I am, to see my glory, which you have given me because you loved me before the foundation of the world. Righteous Father, the world does not know you, but I know you; and these know that you have sent me. I made your name known to them, and I will make it known, so that the love with which you have loved me may be in them, and I in them.
(John 17:20-26 NRSV)

Many young people who desire faithfulness to God are moving away from Christianity because of the condemnation toward the LGBTQ community doled out by various denominations. They want communion with the person of Christ but don't know how to find it within congregations which exclude members based on their sexual or gender identity.

Perhaps even sadder are the millions of atheists who watch this discrimination unfold in Jesus' name. Their derision of faith is confirmed because any being who approves of that behavior while claiming to be the God of love is a liar and a hypocrite.

Today's reading is Jesus' prayer for us, his new church. He prayed for our unity; our supernatural oneness. He has given us the glory the Father passed on to him. He has loved us as the Father loved him. He desires our oneness in return.

To what end? So the world may know God.

The way we demonstrate our oneness with all people—including our LGBTQ friends and family—is the way the world will know we are Christians.

We must never undervalue any person. The workman loves not that his work should be despised in his presence. Now God is present everywhere, and every person is His work.
Saint Francis de Sales

Day 44: Do Justice

Is not this the fast that I choose: to loose the bonds of injustice, to undo the thongs of the yoke, to let the oppressed go free, and to break every yoke? Is it not to share your bread with the hungry, and bring the homeless poor into your house; when you see the naked, to cover them, and not to hide yourself from your own kin? Then your light shall break forth like the dawn, and your healing shall spring up quickly; your vindicator shall go before you, the glory of the Lord shall be your rear guard. Then you shall call, and the Lord will answer; you shall cry for help, and he will say, Here I am. (Isaiah 58:6-9 NRSVCE)

It begins in the Hebrew Scriptures; the lovely picture of what God desires for our behavior as faithful followers of the one who *is* Love.

In Isaiah's day, the Jewish people followed the letter of the law about fasting, but the prophet's words show us it wasn't what God wanted. *His* fast was actions of social justice: to feed the hungry; to free the oppressed; to untie those who are burdened by the yoke of the past; to loose the bonds of injustice.

Members of the LGBTQ community have been oppressed for generations and continue to be oppressed today. They are hunched over, ashamed, denied rights, and excluded. Many are even tortured and killed.

Isaiah repeatedly points to the coming of Jesus, who multiplies these demands for social justice in his own teaching, and who demonstrates them in his actions.

Just look at the promise to those who step up and break apart the bonds and help free the oppressed! Your light shall break forth, healing shall spring up, and God Himself will be your glory and your guard. He will answer your cries for help, and he will be with you:

If you remove the yoke from among you, the accusing finger, and malicious speech; if you lavish your food on the hungry and satisfy the afflicted; then your light shall rise in the darkness, and your gloom shall become like midday; then the Lord will guide you always and satisfy your thirst in

parched places, will give strength to your bones and you shall be like a
watered garden, like a flowing spring whose waters never fail.
(Isaiah 58:9b-11 NABRE)

What glorious promises, just for acting with love and justice toward the LGBTQ people in your life.

Unless we do his teachings, we do not demonstrate faith in him.
Ezra Taft Benson

Day 45: Be Like Children

At that time the disciples came to Jesus, saying, "Who then is greatest in the kingdom of heaven?"

Then Jesus called a little child to Him, set him in the midst of them, and said, "Assuredly, I say to you, unless you are converted and become as little children, you will by no means enter the kingdom of heaven. Therefore whoever humbles himself as this little child is the greatest in the kingdom of heaven. (Matthew 18:1-4 NKJV)

In our enlightened age, we strive to prove our religious worth through knowledge; of scripture, of theology, of many things. We somehow think displaying how much we know shows the sincerity of our faith.

It's this sort of thinking which leads many of us to demand that LGBTQ people have no place in church. We turn to decades of lessons about Bible passages we think prove the idea. As if a particular handful of passages outweigh the very person of God himself; a person which the scriptures show to be radically inclusive and loving. We act like we have inside knowledge and can choose which scriptures outweigh others in order to prove we are insiders.

Jesus tells us this sort of prideful demonstration of knowledge isn't what he wants, and certainly isn't something he requires. Instead, he wants us to approach him like a child. And what are the characteristics of childlike humility? Trust. A desire to lean in and hear. Love. Affection. Faith that you will be cared for.

Not only that; children do not judge people based on what color their skin is, or what country they come from, or who they love. They are accepting of persons until taught otherwise by adults.

So the next time you are tempted to proclaim your knowledge of law, scripture, and "church teaching," remember who Jesus calls us to be; people who have faith in him and who consider everyone a friend. Then be that.

Those who keep speaking about the sun while walking under a cloudy sky are messengers of hope, the true saints of our day.
Henri Nouwen

CALLED TO TRANSFIGURATION

The experience of a loved one coming out to you can be life-changing. You have a choice about the results of that change. Do you want it to culminate in your being angry, bitter, judgmental, and scared, or will you choose instead to become more encouraging, loving, faith-centered, and hopeful? Over our last few days together we'll explore the idea of how being faced with the reality of your loved one's sexual orientation or gender identity has the power to fuel your own transfiguring.

DAY 46: WHAT DOES THE LORD REQUIRE OF YOU?

He has shown you, O mortal, what is good.
And what does the Lord require of you?
To act justly and to love mercy
and to walk humbly with your God. (Micah 6:8 NIV)

The Psalms show us that it's alright to moan and wail to God about the trials we are given in life. News from loved ones about their sexual orientation and gender identity can sometimes feel like too much to bear. It might come on top of financial distress, illness, or all sorts of other stressors, and may drive you to yell at God "What do you want from me?"

The same question may be lifted up to God more calmly, as a genuine request for clarity. You will probably endure conflicting emotions and thoughts about how to properly respond to your loved one. The teaching of your church may counsel separation from the person. Your heart may struggle with anger, confusion, and loss while simultaneously wanting to offer comfort and assurance.

All this is natural, and it is normal to not know quite what to do. But that's okay. Micah tells us that God has shown us what the Lord requires.

God requires us to act justly, to love mercy, and to keep walking humbly with him. Walking humbly means stopping to listen, pray, and ask how to best act with justice and love.

Those are the things God is calling you to today. Those are the things God requires of you.

For there are three ways of performing an act of mercy: the merciful word,
by forgiving, and by comforting; secondly, if you can offer no word, then
pray-that too is mercy; and thirdly, deeds of mercy. And when the Last
Day comes, we shall be judged from this, and on this basis we shall receive
the eternal verdict.
St. Faustina

Day 47: The Refining Fire of God's Calling on our Lives

Beloved, do not be surprised at the fiery trial when it comes upon you to test you, as though something strange were happening to you. But rejoice insofar as you share Christ's sufferings, that you may also rejoice and be glad when his glory is revealed. (1 Peter 4:12-13 ESV)

And some of the wise shall stumble, so that they may be refined, purified, and made white, until the time of the end, for it still awaits the appointed time. (Daniel 11:35 ESV)

Therefore, having been justified by faith, we have peace with God through our Lord Jesus Christ, through whom also we have obtained our introduction by faith into this grace in which we stand; and we exult in hope of the glory of God. And not only this, but we also exult in our tribulations, knowing that tribulation brings about perseverance; and perseverance, proven character; and proven character, hope; and hope does not disappoint, because the love of God has been poured out within our hearts through the Holy Spirit who was given to us.
(Romans 5:1-5 NASB)

Today's passages remind us of the transforming, cleansing power of trials in our lives. Through them we are refined and purified. This happens in a variety of ways. Sometimes we are faced with our own weakness in the face of sickness or suffering. Sometimes we realize how wrong we've been about a situation we thought we understood. Sometimes we are called to rise up out of our addiction; to alcohol, drugs, or even unforgiveness. Sometimes we must deal with regret for not extending love to someone before they died. (In many ways that's the worst of the bunch, because there's nothing that can be done to fix it in this life.)

Trials are a natural part of life. We have a choice to either cooperate with the ways God wants to bring good from them, or to fight them.

Being confronted with a loved one's coming out offers special chances for refinement. Through it, God presents opportunities to be scoured clean from the impurities of pride, judgmentalness, and superiority.

May you take hope in these reassurances; that the trials you face in accepting and embracing loved ones whose identities challenge your understanding of faith can refine you into a closer manifestation of Jesus Christ.

Take hope, but remember; you must cooperate by submitting to the purification.

Out of the fires of refinement, come the praise of His magnificence, the brilliance of His glory, and the honor of His precious Son, Jesus Christ.
Robin Bertram

Day 48: Trust in God's Love of Them

*Are not five sparrows sold for two copper coins? And not one of them is
forgotten before God. But the very hairs of your head are all numbered. Do
not fear therefore; you are of more value than many sparrows.*
(Luke 12:6-7 NKJV)

*Look at the birds of the air, for they neither sow nor reap nor gather into
barns; yet your heavenly Father feeds them. Are you not of more value
than they? Which of you by worrying can add one cubit to his stature?*
(Matthew 6:26-27 NKJV)

Processing news of a loved one's sexual orientation or gender identity
can feel like you are drowning in a sea of confusion and anxiety. It's
particularly hard for parents, whose job throughout the course of
their children's lives is to protect them.

Part of the worry is due to fears about the future. You worry that
they may not be able to find a stable, happy romantic relationship.
You worry that they are angering God. You worry that they'll be the
target of harassment or violence.

Today's readings remind us of how valued we are in the sight of
God. That doesn't mean just the people who follow the letter of
biblical law, or those who go to church every Sunday and tithe 10%.
It means everyone, including your LGBTQ loved one. They are of
much greater value than a whole flock of sparrows. They are made in
the very image of God, and he loves them with his whole being.

Let's take a look at the final verse from the Matthew chapter, just
a few lines after what we read above:

*Therefore do not worry about tomorrow, for tomorrow will worry about its
own things. Sufficient for the day is its own trouble.*
(Matthew 6:34 NKJV)

It may feel like you have many reasons to worry, and of course the
world is full of perils which can make us freeze up when we think
about the vulnerabilities of those we love. But Jesus tells us not to
focus on these worries. And the reason we can rest in this truth is

that God loves those he creates much more than we can possibly love even our most beloved child, family member, or friend.

When we rest in that truth, we have a chance of laying those worries down.

The sin underneath all our sins is to trust the lie of the serpent that we cannot trust the love and grace of Christ and must take matters into our own hands.
Martin Luther

Day 49: Love Covers a Multitude of Sins

*Above all, maintain constant love for one another, for love covers a
multitude of sins. Be hospitable to one another without complaining. Like
good stewards of the manifold grace of God, serve one another with
whatever gift each of you has received. Whoever speaks must do so as one
speaking the very words of God; whoever serves must do so with the
strength that God supplies, so that God may be glorified in all things
through Jesus Christ. To him belong the glory and the power forever and
ever. Amen. (1Peter 4:8-11 NRSV)*

Today's passage is just jam-packed with useful, Godly advice, and the
first line is the most important of them all.

Love covers a multitude of sins.

Jesus is the preeminent example of this, of course; his death
covers all the sin of those who came before us, those living now, and
those who are yet to come. We murdered him, and in response, God
tells us he loves us anyway. What a powerful reminder of how we are
to handle things we perceive as wounds against us and against God.

We are to love.

But the instructions don't stop there. We aren't simply to dole out
a harsh parcel of tough love and turn our backs. We are to be
hospitable, and to serve each other using our gifts.

One of the gifts God has given you is your love for the LGBTQ
person in your life. You felt it before you found out their sexual
orientation or gender identity. You feel it now, despite the pain you
experience along with it. Love is both a gift from God, and a calling
to action.

Here's another verse to remember on this subject:

*As God's chosen ones, holy and beloved, clothe yourselves with compassion,
kindness, humility, meekness, and patience. Bear with one another and, if
anyone has a complaint against another, forgive each other; just as the
Lord has forgiven you, so you also must forgive. Above all, clothe*

yourselves with love, which binds everything together in perfect harmony.
(Colossians 3:12-14 NRSV)

It isn't always easy, to act and serve lovingly. But as today's readings tell us, we don't do it out of our own strength, but with the strength God supplies. And we do it not just for the sake of our loved ones or even ourselves; we do it so that God may be glorified.

Don't be afraid to love your LGBTQ son, daughter, mother, father, friend, brother, sister, or cousin. Love binds everything together in perfect harmony, and God will be glorified when you do.

You are the main character in the story of your life, but other people are the main characters of their own lives. And sometimes you can find healing just by playing a supporting role in someone else's experience.
Timothy Kurek

Day 50: There's Still Time

Let us run with perseverance the race that is set before us, looking to Jesus the pioneer and perfecter of our faith, who for the sake of the joy that was set before him endured the cross, disregarding its shame, and has taken his seat at the right hand of the throne of God. Consider him who endured such hostility against himself from sinners, so that you may not grow weary or lose heart. (Hebrews 12:1b-3 NRSV)

The pain and confusion which arises when a loved one tells you about their sexual orientation or gender identity often stops us from being the loving, nurturing people God calls us to be. It's natural to go through a mourning process, because your idea of who the person was is toppled, and replaced with something which seems foreign to your understanding of them. You may experience a profound sense of loss, and that pain may mean that you speak or act in ways you end up regretting.

If you do handle things badly with your loved one, there's still time to change directions. Healing is possible.

The author of Hebrews describes the faith journey as a race, and a difficult one because while running it, we bear a cross. Our crosses can feel shameful and painful, but we are to keep running. The race is all about our continuous transformation into the image of Christ; a person who loves radically and inclusively, who protects the vulnerable and disdained, and who is angered by those who try to use law to keep people out of heaven.

Part of the race is the never-ending goal of being ambassadors of reconciliation:

All this is from God, who reconciled us to himself through Christ, and has given us the ministry of reconciliation; that is, in Christ God was reconciling the world to himself, not counting their trespasses against them, and entrusting the message of reconciliation to us.
(2 Corinthians 5:18-19 NRSV)

It's natural to behave regrettably while in mourning. But it's never too late to seek peace, and to reconcile with LGBTQ loved ones.

Keep running the race.

A quarrel between friends, when made up, adds a new tie to friendship.
Saint Francis de Sales

CONCLUSION

We've reached the end of our time together, discovering how God wants us to respond to our loved ones' attempt to live full, authentic lives.

If you'd like to continue exploring scripture on these issues, you might want to get *Where True Love Is*; a 90-day devotional which expands on many topics covered here. If your loved one is gender non-conforming, gender queer, or transgender, you can also check out my *Transfigured* devotional.

We are all on this journey through life together. We all face failures and achievements, sorrow and joy, shame and pride. We are all made in God's image, and give God great delight. Let's try to find that delight in the uniqueness of one another, just as God does. Let's try to offer love, healing, and acceptance. Let's try to be encouragers rather than accusers.

By doing so we bring a tiny bit of heaven to earth, here and now.

Why wait?

Made in the USA
Columbia, SC
12 October 2018